I0691157

NO SWEAT GAIN

FITNESS JOURNAL 2016

ACTIVINOTES

Activinotes

DAILY JOURNALS, PLANNERS, NOTEBOOKS AND OTHER BLANK BOOKS

All Rights reserved. No part of this book may be reproduced or used in any way or form or by any means whether electronic or mechanical, this means that you cannot record or photocopy any material ideas or tips that are provided in this book.

Copyright 2016

Date: _____

Aerobic /Cardio			
Exercises	Time/ Distance	Intensity	Calories Burned

Strength			
Exercises	Sets/ Rep	Weight	Rest

Daily Goals					Achieved			
Hours	Minutes	Calories	Weight		Hours	Minutes	Calories	Weight

Nutrition				
Food/Beverage	Calories	Carbs	Fat	Protein

Notes

_____
_____
_____
_____
_____
_____
_____
_____

Date: _____

Aerobic /Cardio

Exercises	Time/ Distance	Intensity	Calories Burned

Strength

Exercises	Sets/ Rep	Weight	Rest

Daily Goals					Achieved			
Hours	Minutes	Calories	Weight		Hours	Minutes	Calories	Weight

Nutrition

Food/Beverage	Calories	Carbs	Fat	Protein

Notes

_____
_____
_____
_____
_____
_____
_____
_____

Date: _____

Aerobic /Cardio

Exercises	Time/ Distance	Intensity	Calories Burned

Strength

Exercises	Sets/ Rep	Weight	Rest

Daily Goals					Achieved			
Hours	Minutes	Calories	Weight		Hours	Minutes	Calories	Weight

Nutrition				
Food/Beverage	Calories	Carbs	Fat	Protein

Notes

_____

_____

_____

_____

_____

_____

_____

_____

Date: _____

Aerobic /Cardio

Exercises	Time/ Distance	Intensity	Calories Burned

Strength

Exercises	Sets/ Rep	Weight	Rest

Daily Goals					Achieved			
Hours	Minutes	Calories	Weight		Hours	Minutes	Calories	Weight

Nutrition

Food/Beverage	Calories	Carbs	Fat	Protein

Notes

_____
_____
_____
_____
_____
_____
_____
_____

Date: _____

Aerobic /Cardio			
Exercises	Time/ Distance	Intensity	Calories Burned

Strength			
Exercises	Sets/ Rep	Weight	Rest

Daily Goals				Achieved			
Hours	Minutes	Calories	Weight	Hours	Minutes	Calories	Weight

Nutrition

Food/Beverage	Calories	Carbs	Fat	Protein

Notes

_____
_____
_____
_____
_____
_____
_____
_____

Date: _____

Aerobic /Cardio

Exercises	Time/ Distance	Intensity	Calories Burned

Strength

Exercises	Sets/ Rep	Weight	Rest

Daily Goals

Hours	Minutes	Calories	Weight

Achieved

Hours	Minutes	Calories	Weight

Nutrition

Food/Beverage	Calories	Carbs	Fat	Protein

Notes

_____
_____
_____
_____
_____
_____
_____
_____

Date: _____

Aerobic /Cardio			
Exercises	Time/ Distance	Intensity	Calories Burned

Strength			
Exercises	Sets/ Rep	Weight	Rest

Daily Goals					Achieved			
Hours	Minutes	Calories	Weight		Hours	Minutes	Calories	Weight

Nutrition

Food/Beverage	Calories	Carbs	Fat	Protein

Notes

_____

_____

_____

_____

_____

_____

_____

_____

Date: _____

Aerobic /Cardio			
Exercises	Time/ Distance	Intensity	Calories Burned

Strength			
Exercises	Sets/ Rep	Weight	Rest

Daily Goals

Hours	Minutes	Calories	Weight

Achieved

Hours	Minutes	Calories	Weight

Nutrition

Food/Beverage	Calories	Carbs	Fat	Protein

Notes

_____
_____
_____
_____
_____
_____
_____
_____

Date: _____

Aerobic /Cardio

Exercises	Time/ Distance	Intensity	Calories Burned

Strength

Exercises	Sets/ Rep	Weight	Rest

Daily Goals					Achieved			
Hours	Minutes	Calories	Weight		Hours	Minutes	Calories	Weight

Nutrition

Food/Beverage	Calories	Carbs	Fat	Protein

Notes

_____
_____
_____
_____
_____
_____
_____
_____

Date: _____

Aerobic /Cardio

Exercises	Time/ Distance	Intensity	Calories Burned

Strength

Exercises	Sets/ Rep	Weight	Rest

Daily Goals

Hours	Minutes	Calories	Weight

Achieved

Hours	Minutes	Calories	Weight

Nutrition

Food/Beverage	Calories	Carbs	Fat	Protein

Notes

_____
_____
_____
_____
_____
_____
_____
_____

Date: _____

Aerobic /Cardio

Exercises	Time/ Distance	Intensity	Calories Burned

Strength

Exercises	Sets/ Rep	Weight	Rest

Daily Goals					Achieved			
Hours	Minutes	Calories	Weight		Hours	Minutes	Calories	Weight

Nutrition

Food/Beverage	Calories	Carbs	Fat	Protein

Notes

_____
_____
_____
_____
_____
_____
_____
_____

Date: _____

Aerobic /Cardio			
Exercises	Time/ Distance	Intensity	Calories Burned

Strength			
Exercises	Sets/ Rep	Weight	Rest

Daily Goals

Hours	Minutes	Calories	Weight

Achieved

Hours	Minutes	Calories	Weight

Nutrition

Food/Beverage	Calories	Carbs	Fat	Protein

Notes

_____

_____

_____

_____

_____

_____

_____

Date: _____

Aerobic /Cardio			
Exercises	Time/ Distance	Intensity	Calories Burned

Strength			
Exercises	Sets/ Rep	Weight	Rest

Daily Goals				Achieved			
Hours	Minutes	Calories	Weight	Hours	Minutes	Calories	Weight

Nutrition

Food/Beverage	Calories	Carbs	Fat	Protein

Notes

_____

_____

_____

_____

_____

_____

_____

_____

_____

Date: _____

Aerobic /Cardio			
Exercises	Time/ Distance	Intensity	Calories Burned

Strength			
Exercises	Sets/ Rep	Weight	Rest

Daily Goals

Hours	Minutes	Calories	Weight

Achieved

Hours	Minutes	Calories	Weight

Nutrition

Food/Beverage	Calories	Carbs	Fat	Protein

Notes

_____
_____
_____
_____
_____
_____
_____
_____

Date: _____

Aerobic /Cardio

Exercises	Time/ Distance	Intensity	Calories Burned

Strength

Exercises	Sets/ Rep	Weight	Rest

Daily Goals					Achieved			
Hours	Minutes	Calories	Weight		Hours	Minutes	Calories	Weight

Nutrition

Food/Beverage	Calories	Carbs	Fat	Protein

Notes

_____

_____

_____

_____

_____

_____

_____

_____

Date: _____

Aerobic /Cardio

Exercises	Time/ Distance	Intensity	Calories Burned

Strength

Exercises	Sets/ Rep	Weight	Rest

Daily Goals

Hours	Minutes	Calories	Weight

Achieved

Hours	Minutes	Calories	Weight

Nutrition

Food/Beverage	Calories	Carbs	Fat	Protein

Notes

_____
_____
_____
_____
_____
_____
_____
_____

Date: _____

Aerobic /Cardio			
Exercises	Time/ Distance	Intensity	Calories Burned

Strength			
Exercises	Sets/ Rep	Weight	Rest

Daily Goals

Hours	Minutes	Calories	Weight

Achieved

Hours	Minutes	Calories	Weight

Nutrition

Food/Beverage	Calories	Carbs	Fat	Protein

Notes

_____
_____
_____
_____
_____
_____
_____
_____

Date: _____

Aerobic /Cardio			
Exercises	Time/ Distance	Intensity	Calories Burned

Strength			
Exercises	Sets/ Rep	Weight	Rest

Daily Goals

Hours	Minutes	Calories	Weight

Achieved

Hours	Minutes	Calories	Weight

Nutrition

Food/Beverage	Calories	Carbs	Fat	Protein

Notes

_____
_____
_____
_____
_____
_____
_____
_____

Date: _____

Aerobic /Cardio			
Exercises	Time/ Distance	Intensity	Calories Burned

Strength			
Exercises	Sets/ Rep	Weight	Rest

Daily Goals					Achieved			
Hours	Minutes	Calories	Weight		Hours	Minutes	Calories	Weight

Nutrition				
Food/Beverage	Calories	Carbs	Fat	Protein

Notes

_____
_____
_____
_____
_____
_____
_____
_____

Date: _____

Aerobic /Cardio			
Exercises	Time/ Distance	Intensity	Calories Burned

Strength			
Exercises	Sets/ Rep	Weight	Rest

Daily Goals				Achieved			
Hours	Minutes	Calories	Weight	Hours	Minutes	Calories	Weight

Nutrition				
Food/Beverage	Calories	Carbs	Fat	Protein

Notes

_____
_____
_____
_____
_____
_____
_____
_____

Date: _____

Aerobic /Cardio			
Exercises	Time/ Distance	Intensity	Calories Burned

Strength			
Exercises	Sets/ Rep	Weight	Rest

Daily Goals					Achieved			
Hours	Minutes	Calories	Weight		Hours	Minutes	Calories	Weight

Nutrition				
Food/Beverage	Calories	Carbs	Fat	Protein

Notes

_____

_____

_____

_____

_____

_____

_____

_____

Date: _____

Aerobic /Cardio			
Exercises	Time/ Distance	Intensity	Calories Burned

Strength			
Exercises	Sets/ Rep	Weight	Rest

Daily Goals

Hours	Minutes	Calories	Weight

Achieved

Hours	Minutes	Calories	Weight

Nutrition

Food/Beverage	Calories	Carbs	Fat	Protein

Notes

_____
_____
_____
_____
_____
_____
_____
_____

Date: _____

Aerobic /Cardio			
Exercises	Time/ Distance	Intensity	Calories Burned

Strength			
Exercises	Sets/ Rep	Weight	Rest

Daily Goals					Achieved			
Hours	Minutes	Calories	Weight		Hours	Minutes	Calories	Weight

Nutrition

Food/Beverage	Calories	Carbs	Fat	Protein

Notes

_____
_____
_____
_____
_____
_____
_____
_____

Date: _____

Aerobic /Cardio			
Exercises	Time/ Distance	Intensity	Calories Burned

Strength			
Exercises	Sets/ Rep	Weight	Rest

Daily Goals					Achieved			
Hours	Minutes	Calories	Weight		Hours	Minutes	Calories	Weight

Nutrition				
Food/Beverage	Calories	Carbs	Fat	Protein

Notes

_____
_____
_____
_____
_____
_____
_____
_____

Date: _____

Aerobic /Cardio			
Exercises	Time/ Distance	Intensity	Calories Burned

Strength			
Exercises	Sets/ Rep	Weight	Rest

Daily Goals					Achieved			
Hours	Minutes	Calories	Weight		Hours	Minutes	Calories	Weight

Nutrition				
Food/Beverage	Calories	Carbs	Fat	Protein

Notes

_____
_____
_____
_____
_____
_____
_____
_____

Date: _____

Aerobic /Cardio			
Exercises	Time/ Distance	Intensity	Calories Burned

Strength			
Exercises	Sets/ Rep	Weight	Rest

Daily Goals

Hours	Minutes	Calories	Weight

Achieved

Hours	Minutes	Calories	Weight

Nutrition

Food/Beverage	Calories	Carbs	Fat	Protein

Notes

_____
_____
_____
_____
_____
_____
_____
_____

Date: _____

Aerobic /Cardio			
Exercises	Time/ Distance	Intensity	Calories Burned

Strength			
Exercises	Sets/ Rep	Weight	Rest

Daily Goals					Achieved			
Hours	Minutes	Calories	Weight		Hours	Minutes	Calories	Weight

Nutrition				
Food/Beverage	Calories	Carbs	Fat	Protein

Notes

_____
_____
_____
_____
_____
_____
_____
_____

Date: _____

Aerobic /Cardio			
Exercises	Time/ Distance	Intensity	Calories Burned

Strength			
Exercises	Sets/ Rep	Weight	Rest

Daily Goals					Achieved			
Hours	Minutes	Calories	Weight		Hours	Minutes	Calories	Weight

Nutrition

Food/Beverage	Calories	Carbs	Fat	Protein

Notes

_____
_____
_____
_____
_____
_____
_____
_____

Date: _____

Aerobic /Cardio

Exercises	Time/ Distance	Intensity	Calories Burned

Strength

Exercises	Sets/ Rep	Weight	Rest

Daily Goals

Hours	Minutes	Calories	Weight

Achieved

Hours	Minutes	Calories	Weight

Nutrition

Food/Beverage	Calories	Carbs	Fat	Protein

Notes

_____

_____

_____

_____

_____

_____

_____

_____

Date: _____

Aerobic /Cardio			
Exercises	Time/ Distance	Intensity	Calories Burned

Strength			
Exercises	Sets/ Rep	Weight	Rest

Daily Goals

Hours	Minutes	Calories	Weight

Achieved

Hours	Minutes	Calories	Weight

Nutrition

Food/Beverage	Calories	Carbs	Fat	Protein

Notes

_____
_____
_____
_____
_____
_____
_____
_____

Date: _____

Aerobic /Cardio			
Exercises	Time/ Distance	Intensity	Calories Burned

Strength			
Exercises	Sets/ Rep	Weight	Rest

Daily Goals

Hours	Minutes	Calories	Weight

Achieved

Hours	Minutes	Calories	Weight

Nutrition

Food/Beverage	Calories	Carbs	Fat	Protein

Notes

_____
_____
_____
_____
_____
_____
_____
_____

Date: _____

Aerobic /Cardio			
Exercises	Time/ Distance	Intensity	Calories Burned

Strength			
Exercises	Sets/ Rep	Weight	Rest

Daily Goals

Hours	Minutes	Calories	Weight

Achieved

Hours	Minutes	Calories	Weight

Nutrition

Food/Beverage	Calories	Carbs	Fat	Protein

Notes

_____
_____
_____
_____
_____
_____
_____
_____

Date: _____

Aerobic /Cardio			
Exercises	Time/ Distance	Intensity	Calories Burned

Strength			
Exercises	Sets/ Rep	Weight	Rest

Daily Goals

Hours	Minutes	Calories	Weight

Achieved

Hours	Minutes	Calories	Weight

Nutrition

Food/Beverage	Calories	Carbs	Fat	Protein

Notes

_____
_____
_____
_____
_____
_____
_____
_____

Date: _____

Aerobic /Cardio			
Exercises	Time/ Distance	Intensity	Calories Burned

Strength			
Exercises	Sets/ Rep	Weight	Rest

Daily Goals					Achieved			
Hours	Minutes	Calories	Weight		Hours	Minutes	Calories	Weight

Nutrition				
Food/Beverage	Calories	Carbs	Fat	Protein

Notes

_____
_____
_____
_____
_____
_____
_____
_____

Date: _____

Aerobic /Cardio			
Exercises	Time/ Distance	Intensity	Calories Burned

Strength			
Exercises	Sets/ Rep	Weight	Rest

Daily Goals					Achieved			
Hours	Minutes	Calories	Weight		Hours	Minutes	Calories	Weight

Nutrition

Food/Beverage	Calories	Carbs	Fat	Protein

Notes

_____
_____
_____
_____
_____
_____
_____
_____

Date: _____

Aerobic /Cardio			
Exercises	Time/ Distance	Intensity	Calories Burned

Strength			
Exercises	Sets/ Rep	Weight	Rest

Daily Goals					Achieved			
Hours	Minutes	Calories	Weight		Hours	Minutes	Calories	Weight

Nutrition

Food/Beverage	Calories	Carbs	Fat	Protein

Notes

_____
_____
_____
_____
_____
_____
_____
_____

Date: _____

Aerobic /Cardio			
Exercises	Time/ Distance	Intensity	Calories Burned

Strength			
Exercises	Sets/ Rep	Weight	Rest

Daily Goals					Achieved			
Hours	Minutes	Calories	Weight		Hours	Minutes	Calories	Weight

Nutrition

Food/Beverage	Calories	Carbs	Fat	Protein

Notes

_____
_____
_____
_____
_____
_____
_____
_____

Date: _____

Aerobic /Cardio			
Exercises	Time/ Distance	Intensity	Calories Burned

Strength			
Exercises	Sets/ Rep	Weight	Rest

Daily Goals					Achieved			
Hours	Minutes	Calories	Weight		Hours	Minutes	Calories	Weight

Nutrition				
Food/Beverage	Calories	Carbs	Fat	Protein

Notes

_____
_____
_____
_____
_____
_____
_____
_____

Date: _____

Aerobic /Cardio			
Exercises	Time/ Distance	Intensity	Calories Burned

Strength			
Exercises	Sets/ Rep	Weight	Rest

Daily Goals

Hours	Minutes	Calories	Weight

Achieved

Hours	Minutes	Calories	Weight

Nutrition

Food/Beverage	Calories	Carbs	Fat	Protein

Notes

Date: _____

Aerobic /Cardio			
Exercises	Time/ Distance	Intensity	Calories Burned

Strength			
Exercises	Sets/ Rep	Weight	Rest

Daily Goals

Hours	Minutes	Calories	Weight

Achieved

Hours	Minutes	Calories	Weight

Nutrition

Food/Beverage	Calories	Carbs	Fat	Protein

Notes

_____
_____
_____
_____
_____
_____
_____
_____

Date: _____

Aerobic /Cardio			
Exercises	Time/ Distance	Intensity	Calories Burned

Strength			
Exercises	Sets/ Rep	Weight	Rest

Daily Goals					Achieved			
Hours	Minutes	Calories	Weight		Hours	Minutes	Calories	Weight

Nutrition				
Food/Beverage	Calories	Carbs	Fat	Protein

Notes

_____
_____
_____
_____
_____
_____
_____
_____

Date: _____

Aerobic /Cardio			
Exercises	Time/ Distance	Intensity	Calories Burned

Strength			
Exercises	Sets/ Rep	Weight	Rest

Daily Goals					Achieved			
Hours	Minutes	Calories	Weight		Hours	Minutes	Calories	Weight

Nutrition				
Food/Beverage	Calories	Carbs	Fat	Protein

Notes

_____
_____
_____
_____
_____
_____
_____
_____

Date: _____

Aerobic /Cardio			
Exercises	Time/ Distance	Intensity	Calories Burned

Strength			
Exercises	Sets/ Rep	Weight	Rest

Daily Goals					Achieved			
Hours	Minutes	Calories	Weight		Hours	Minutes	Calories	Weight

Nutrition

Food/Beverage	Calories	Carbs	Fat	Protein

Notes

_____
_____
_____
_____
_____
_____
_____
_____

Date: _____

Aerobic /Cardio

Exercises	Time/ Distance	Intensity	Calories Burned

Strength

Exercises	Sets/ Rep	Weight	Rest

Daily Goals

Hours	Minutes	Calories	Weight

Achieved

Hours	Minutes	Calories	Weight

Nutrition

Food/Beverage	Calories	Carbs	Fat	Protein

Notes

_____
_____
_____
_____
_____
_____
_____
_____

Date: _____

Aerobic /Cardio			
Exercises	Time/ Distance	Intensity	Calories Burned

Strength			
Exercises	Sets/ Rep	Weight	Rest

Daily Goals					Achieved			
Hours	Minutes	Calories	Weight		Hours	Minutes	Calories	Weight

Nutrition				
Food/Beverage	Calories	Carbs	Fat	Protein

Notes

_____
_____
_____
_____
_____
_____
_____
_____

Date: _____

Aerobic / Cardio			
Exercises	Time/ Distance	Intensity	Calories Burned

Strength			
Exercises	Sets/ Rep	Weight	Rest

Daily Goals					Achieved			
Hours	Minutes	Calories	Weight		Hours	Minutes	Calories	Weight

Nutrition				
Food/Beverage	Calories	Carbs	Fat	Protein

Notes

_____
_____
_____
_____
_____
_____
_____
_____

Date: _____

Aerobic /Cardio			
Exercises	Time/ Distance	Intensity	Calories Burned

Strength			
Exercises	Sets/ Rep	Weight	Rest

Daily Goals					Achieved			
Hours	Minutes	Calories	Weight		Hours	Minutes	Calories	Weight

Nutrition

Food/Beverage	Calories	Carbs	Fat	Protein

Notes

_____

_____

_____

_____

_____

_____

_____

_____

Date: _____

Aerobic /Cardio			
Exercises	Time/ Distance	Intensity	Calories Burned

Strength			
Exercises	Sets/ Rep	Weight	Rest

Daily Goals				Achieved			
Hours	Minutes	Calories	Weight	Hours	Minutes	Calories	Weight

Nutrition

Food/Beverage	Calories	Carbs	Fat	Protein

Notes

_____
_____
_____
_____
_____
_____
_____
_____

Date: _____

Aerobic /Cardio			
Exercises	Time/ Distance	Intensity	Calories Burned

Strength			
Exercises	Sets/ Rep	Weight	Rest

Daily Goals					Achieved			
Hours	Minutes	Calories	Weight		Hours	Minutes	Calories	Weight

Nutrition

Food/Beverage	Calories	Carbs	Fat	Protein

Notes

_____
_____
_____
_____
_____
_____
_____
_____

www.ingramcontent.com/pod-product-compliance
Lightning Source LLC
Chambersburg PA
CBHW080739250626
47170CB00010B/2886